3-7

PENGUIN MODERN EUROPEAN POETS
Advisory Editor: A. Alvarez
D95

MIROSLAV HOLUB
Selected Poems

Selected Poems

MIROSLAV HOLUB, 1923-

TRANSLATED BY
Ian Milner and George Theiner

WITH AN INTRODUCTION BY
A. ALVAREZ

PENGUIN BOOKS
BALTIMORE · MARYLAND

Penguin Books Ltd, Harmondsworth, Middlesex, England
Penguin Books Inc., 3300 Clipper Mill Road, Baltimore 11, Md, U.S.A.
Penguin Books Australia Ltd, Ringwood, Victoria, Australia

—

First published 1967

—

—

Made and printed in Great Britain
by Cox & Wyman Ltd,
London, Fakenham and Reading
Set in Monotype Garamond

A-T

Contents

PART THREE

PART FOUR

Acknowledgements

Certain of the translations in this book first appeared in the following publications: the *Observer, The Times Literary Supplement, New Zealand Monthly Review, Universum, Czechoslovak Life, Overland* and *Landfall.*

Introduction to the poetry of Miroslav Holub

Miroslav Holub is a curious mixture, perhaps a unique one: he is one of Czechoslovakia's most prolific and original poets and also a distinguished scientist, a clinical pathologist who has travelled widely on both sides of the Iron Curtain, researching and attending scientific congresses. So far his publications include eight books of poetry, two travel books and twenty-five learned papers on pathology; he also edits a Czech popular science magazine.

The combination of poetry and science is not altogether unprecedented; Lucretius made experiments of a kind, so did Goethe; and then there was Erasmus Darwin who versified *The Lives of the Plants*. What makes Holub so unusual is his distinction in both fields. When scientists turn to verse the results usually resemble the poems of that eminent Cambridge physicist, the late Professor Andrade: elegant in their old-fashioned way, but over-mellow, coy, soft at the centre, a sentimental Mr Hyde to his formidable Dr Jekyll. The gloomy general rule seems to be that, even with the best will in the world, the split between the two cultures is radical, if only because the scientists won't take the discipline of the arts seriously. So they go to poetry simply as a *relief* from the intellectual stringency and sophistication of their professions.

Nothing could be less true of Holub's work. I do not know – and if I did, could not judge – the intellectual qualities that distinguish him as a scientist. But I imagine they have much in common with the subtlety and precision of his poetry, and with the openness to experience which so continually informs and controls it. If Holub remains a scientist in his verse, it is not because he is dry or schematic, dogmatic or aggressively intellectual; it is, instead, because he is always experimental. According to Karl Popper, the basis of every scientific law is the principle of falsifiability: a law, that is, is valid only if it can be, but has not been, disproved. Holub seems to write his poems as though with that in mind; his attitude is tentative, empirical, alert.

Born in 1923, the son of a railway worker and a language teacher, Holub did not begin to write poems until he started his clinical research at the age of about thirty. So experimental science and experimental verse have flowered together throughout his career. When I met him last in Prague, I asked him if he had any poetic theories I should know about. He came back the next day with a couple of pages of typescript with a characteristic heading: 'Some very individual points/valid on June 8th, 1965, 17.00 hrs.' The fourth of these eleven points was this:

There is no deep difference between the scientific mind and the artistic mind: both include the maximal creativity with the maximal freedom. Science is both theoretic and experimental. Art is only experimental.

The heart of the matter is the word 'experimental': he was, I believe, referring more to the content than to shape and technique of verse; or rather, since these elements cannot be separated, the stress is on what the poem is saying rather than how it says it. Granted, the form of Holub's work is strenuously anti-traditional; he invariably uses the freest of free verse, and has employed in his time some elaborate tricks to break down the purely literary limitations of poetry (I will come back to these). But that, in a way, is only a part of a traditional battle perennially fought in Czech verse between the lyrical romantics and the analytic poets. So as the foremost 'analyst' Holub belongs to a tradition of anti-traditional writers. The real experimentation in his verse is not a question of new literary devices, but of the use of *anti-literary* devices to evolve a form that is flexible enough to take any kind of experience or pressure as it comes. And for Holub, 'experience' includes, or is defined by, the scientist's energy, cunning and sharpness.

Seen in one light, the whole of the modern movement, from the turn of the century up to the present, has been concerned with the problem of extending the possible range of the arts, with breaking down conventional responses and expectations, and working out forms to express whatever the present urgencies are felt to be. But in general, the movement the arts have taken has been inward: poets and painters have become more and more concerned with exploring the extreme edge of the viable, with harnessing in their work the insights and energy released by breakdown, neurosis, paranoia, despair and drugs. In its way, Holub's poetry is no less exploratory than that of the Extremist poets of the West, but it takes the opposite direction. His business is with the way in which private responses, private anxieties, connect up with the public world of science, technology and machines, with the way, as he said in an interview on Prague Radio, we put out 'tips into this world of scooters, skyscrapers and streptomycin'.

Perhaps this is inevitable, since he is a Marxist. But his Marxism is in no sense dogmatic or party biased. Poems like 'Polonius' and 'Discobolus' – indeed, most of the third section of this book – are sharply against the Establishment, with its attendant bureaucrats and manœuvrer. His politics, no less than the rest of his work, is continually exposed to that tension between theory and experienced reality which he calls 'experiment'. For example, the whole point of the long poem 'The Root of the Matter' is to set life as it is lived in the feelings and senses against the slogans and clichés through which you must continually thread your way.

> Some mistakes are now mistakes
> others are still virtues

That could stand as the ironic motto for the whole of post-Stalinist Czechoslovakia.

Perhaps the key to what he is after as a political-scientist-poet is to be found in poems like 'Pathology', or 'In the Microscope':

> Here too are dreaming landscapes,
> lunar, derelict.
> Here too are the masses
> tillers of the soil.
> And cells, fighters
> who lay down their lives
> for a song.
>
> Here too are cemeteries,
> fame and snow.
> And I hear murmuring,
> the revolt of immense estates.

It is a kind of embattled Communist Party vision of the world reduced to microscopic dimensions; and thereby judged ironically; and thereby also dignified. For this scaling down of politics by means of science is not done for the sake of satire but for the sake of proportion. The final standard is a sense of common humanity; and in the final analysis science is just one among many of the human gifts, like the gift of curiosity or inventiveness or creativity or patience, or a gratuitous gift like love:

> We have
> a map of the universe
> for microbes,
> we have a map of a microbe
> for the universe.
>
> We have
> a Grand Master of chess
> made of electronic circuits.

But above all
we have
the ability to sort peas,
to cup water in our hands,
to seek
the right screw
under the sofa
for hours

This
gives us
wings.

('Wings')

In the light of this kind of writing it is as meaningless to call
Holub a humanist as it is to call him a Marxist; for both terms
imply a programme and dogma, even if, for the humanist, they are only the vague programmes and vaguer dogmas
of optimistic liberalism. Holub's poems are rooted in something harder and more empirical than that: in a resistant,
decent, unbelieving sense of the realities of people and their
troubles. If he seems optimistic, it is only with the practical,
untheoretical optimism of the scientist who is kept going
through all the dragging boredom of an experiment by the
hope somewhere of a genuinely new result.

This is where the experimental poet joins with the
experimental scientist: common to both is a sense of discovery. But where the pathologist makes his discoveries in
his specialized field, the poet makes them about feelings,
about situations, about a shared, troubled humanity. At the
core of both is a wary, critical, open attitude to experience.
Thus science and poetry become two ways of looking at
the same reality, differing only in technique:

There are [runs the third of Holub's 'very individual points'] no
different realities. What can be created by art is not a new reality,
but a deeper approach to the intrinsic and extrinsic facts of

human life. These facts are the kingdom of the arts and philosophy only to that moment when they become accessible to scientific methods.

All Holub's technique is concentrated on the exposure and analysis of reality. He speaks fluent English, reads widely in it, and claims to have derived his free verse forms from William Carlos Williams. But the results are very different. Williams used his simple, stripped-down forms for two purposes: first, to achieve an American accent and rhythm, which had nothing to do with the traditional British iambic pentameter; second, in order to make the rather simple perceptions and objects of his poems come out clear and strong. Complexity was not his *forte*, and when he attempted it the result, as often as not, was muddle. Holub, in comparison, is intellectual, sophisticated. Consider, for example, 'Love':

> Two thousand cigarettes.
> A hundred miles
> from wall to wall.
> An eternity and a half of vigils
> blanker than snow.
>
> Tons of words
> old as the tracks
> of a platypus in the sand.
>
> A hundred books we didn't write.
> A hundred pyramids we didn't build.
>
> Sweepings.
> Dust.
>
> Bitter
> as a beginning of the world.
>
> Believe me when I say
> it was beautiful.

The technique is that of the early abstract painters: he reduces the confused, uneasy situation to its bare elements, and then reassembles it so that the complexity is somehow clarified, validated by an ironic compassion. He uses free forms so that they won't get in the way of what he has to say. They allow him complexity without padding. And this is as it should be for an intellectual who has no taste for abstractions. In his poetry, as presumably in his science, he continually insists on probing below the surface of received, everyday experience to reveal new levels of meaning, to lay bare new emotional facts. It is as though his poems and his researcher's microscope worked in the same way, and towards the same end.

It is in this realm of at once confirming and extending reality that he has made some of his most fruitful experiments. He is much concerned with widening the potential audience of poetry. As he said in the Prague Radio interview:

Most of all I like writing for people untouched by poetry; for instance, for those who do not even know that it should at all be for them. I would like them to read poems as naturally as they read the papers, or go to a football game. Not to consider it as anything more difficult, or effeminate, or praiseworthy.

If this is in part the good Marxist speaking, the results have nothing at all to do with the inert, pedantic code of 'socialist realism'. Holub has experimented with what he calls 'synthetic art. Poetry plus music plus pictures plus I know not what'. This is in line with the work of another brilliant Czech artist, the stage designer Josef Svoboda, who in his *Magic Lantern* and in many of his productions at the National Theatre has cunningly fused live theatre with the cinema. Holub's attempts at synthesis have been made in collaboration with a young photographer, Jan Pařík, whose chief subject is life in hospital wards and operating theatres. Holub's poems begin where the photographs leave off, they are meditations which go, in his own words, 'beyond them and behind them'. (A number of poems in the first section, such as 'The Harp', 'Reality', 'Great and Strong', are free variations on Pařík's photographs.) Behind them all is an attempt to make people think about what they experience from day to day, to make them connect up what they see with what they read and feel.

This refusal to separate modern life into neat, isolated compartments is fundamental to all Holub's work, and to his importance. In the second of his 'points' he remarks:

Art has to be the product of a complete personality aware of all information and assumptions valid for the citizen of the modern world. Superstitious exclusion of science from arts and humanities does not preserve creativity; it preserves only old approaches and old reactions, which become more and more confused in the modern world.

This, I think, cuts through a good deal of the muddle which plagues discussion of the modern arts, a muddle about traditional values and the contemporary situation. When, for example, the Leavisites assert that there is a total discrepancy between mass society and minority culture, or the American existentialists insist on the equally total 'alienation' of the artist from his technological consumer society, both are on to a partial truth; but for the sake of it they are denying whatever is positive and hopeful in the industrial, electronic world. Both are, in some degree, rejecting what we have, in favour of a tense nostalgia for what we have lost. No doubt, what has been lost was very valuable; no doubt, the close-knit, mutually self-supporting, pre-industrial-revolution communities had a strength and assurance that our own lack. But they had also ceased to exist at least by 1918, probably long before. To lament their passing may be right and proper, but utterly to reject what has taken their place is mere conservative utopianism. It is, after all, difficult to feel deprived of what one never knew.

This is not a trap Holub has ever fallen into. On the contrary, the source of his strength is his subtle, critical acceptance of the realities as they are, his refusal either to shut things out or to praise them simply because, like Everest, they are there. His poetry is based finally on an unsentimental, probing, compassionate, witty sense of the modern world. As he says in 'The Root of the Matter':

> There is poetry in everything. That
> is the biggest argument
> against poetry.

A. Alvarez.

PART ONE

A Helping Hand

We gave a helping hand to grass –
  and it turned into corn.
We gave a helping hand to fire –
  and it turned into a rocket.
Hesitatingly,
cautiously,
we give a helping hand
to people,
to some people . . .

Bones

We lay aside
   useless bones,
   ribs of reptiles,
   jawbones of cats,
   the hip-bone of the storm,
   the wish-bone of Fate.

   To prop the growing head
   of Man
We seek
   a backbone
   that will stay
   straight.

Wings

We have
a microscopic anatomy
of the whale
this
gives
Man
assurance

*William Carlos
Williams*

We have
a map of the universe
for microbes,
we have
a map of a microbe
for the universe.

We have
a Grand Master of chess
made of electronic circuits.

But above all
we have
the ability
to sort peas,
to cup water in our hands,
to seek
the right screw
under the sofa
for hours

This
gives us
wings.

'Heat with a Little Human Warmth'

They take
a bit of the world,
put it
in a pan,
heat it,
stew it
in its own juice,
listen
to the fervent sizzling.

All their life
they wait
for the fried meat-ball.

But under that lid
there are
equations,
frost
and flames.

In the Microscope

Here too are dreaming landscapes,
lunar, derelict.
Here too are the masses
tillers of the soil.
And cells, fighters
who lay down their lives
for a song.

Here too are cemeteries,
fame and snow.
And I hear murmuring,
the revolt of immense estates.

Reality

The small worms of pain still wriggled
   in the limpid air,
The trembling died away and
Something in us bowed low before
   the fact of the operating-table
   the fact of the window
   the fact of space
   the fact of steel
   with seven blades.

The silence was inviolable
   like the surface of a mirror.

Though we wanted to ask
Where the blood was flowing
And
Whether you were still dead,
   darling.

Suffering

Ugly creatures, ugly grunting creatures,
Completely concealed under the point of the needle,
 behind the curve of the Research Task Graph,
Disgusting creatures with foam at the mouth,
 with bristles on their bottoms,
One after the other
They close their pink mouths
They open their pink mouths
They grow pale
Flutter their legs
 as if they were running a very
 long distance,

They close ugly blue eyes,
They open ugly blue eyes
 and
 they're
 dead.

But I ask no questions,
no one asks any questions.

And after their death we let the ugly creatures
 run in pieces along the white expanse
 of the paper electrophore
We let them graze in the greenish-blue pool
 of the chromatogram
And in pieces we drive them for a dip
 in alcohol
 and xylol
And the immense eye of the ugly animal god
 watches their every move
 through the tube of the microscope

And the bits of animals are satisfied
like flowers in a flower-pot
   like kittens at the bottom of a pond
   like cells before conception.
But I ask no questions,
   no one asks any questions,
Naturally no one asks
Whether these creatures wouldn't have preferred
   to live all in one piece,
   their disgusting life
   in bogs
   and canals,
Whether they wouldn't have preferred to eat
   one another alive,
Whether they wouldn't have preferred to make love
   in between horror and hunger,
Whether they wouldn't have preferred to use
   all their eyes and pores to perceive
   their muddy stinking little world
Incredibly terrified,
Incredibly happy
In the way of matter which can do no more.

But I ask no questions,
   no one asks any questions,
Because it's all quite useless,
Experiments succeed and experiments fail,
Like everything else in this world,
   in which the truth advances
   like some splendid silver bulldozer
   in the tumbling darkness,

Like everything else in this world,
   in which I met a lonely girl
   inside a shop selling bridal veils,

In which I met a general covered
  with oak leaves,
In which I met ambulance men who could find no
  wounded,
In which I met a man who had lost
  his name,
In which I met a glorious and famous, bronze,
  incredibly terrified rat,
In which I met people who wanted to lay down
  their lives and people who wanted to lay down
  their heads in sorrow,
In which, come to think of it, I keep meeting my
  own self at every step.

Pathology

Here in the Lord's bosom rest
the tongues of beggars,
the lungs of generals,
the eyes of informers,
the skins of martyrs,

in the absolute
of the microscope's lenses.

I leaf through Old Testament slices of liver,
in the white monuments of brain I read
the hieroglyphs
of decay.

Behold, Christians,
Heaven, Hell, and Paradise
in bottles.
And no wailing,
not even a sigh.
Only the dust moans.
Dumb is history
strained
through capillaries.

Equality dumb. Fraternity dumb.

And out of the tricolours of mortal suffering
we day after day
pull
threads of wisdom.

Silence

Garlands of fatted words are strung through the city
   from mouth to mouth,
Since spring the voices have blared from pillar to post
   and now pitch on the shoulders of autumn,
The youths babble their birdshit in the official ear,
   nothing venture nothing win,
And eight Hail Marys have coaxed a calf
   out of a barren cow.

The ton-heavy drone of voices climbs
   to the first heaven.
But despite the cock-a-doodle-doo, despite
   the bogeymen of the woods and lip-smacking devourers
   of dried butterflies,
In the beginning and the end silence
   endures like a knife,
The silence drawn from the sheath at the moment
   when we have our backs
   to the last wall,
When we lean upon
   nothing but the green breath of the sea,
When we lean upon
   the sheer weight of the earth,
When we lean upon
   ourselves alone,
Screened by our sweat from words.

It is the silence we learn
   the whole of a lifetime,
The silence in which you hear
   a small boy
   ask deep within,
What do you think, mum?

The Harp

Of all stringed instruments I like best
   the harp stretched from hand to hand,
From blood to blood. From disaster to deliverance. From
   error to perfection.
Of all stringed instruments I like best
   the harp of healing.
Its music sounds at man's deep centre.
And King David plays it,
He who never was,
He who always will be when the candle
   gutters and the flesh
   is lifting off the bone.

Great and Strong

A little blood, more or less, he said,
He was great and strong, so strong
   it must have been from weakness,
A little blood, he said, and went to wash his hands,
Of course there are things you can't wash off,
But that he didn't know, for he was strong,
He was smart with his elbows, then used his fists,
When he spoke he guzzled the words of others,
The seeing air was stunned and the ant-swarm
   of the transistors crawled through his ears,
A little blood, this man said and
   instantly his words were the thoughts of all,
It was he who conquered at Carthage,
Clean as the map of an unnecessary battle,
Clean as the anatomy of a hyena,
Clean as the conscience of a gun,
Clean as the hands that run a slaughter-house,
Clean as the king of the ants,
Pure as the sperm of Genghis Khan,
Clean as the spore of anthrax,
Clean as the bare behind of death,
All bent their heads,
The tampons bowed to him
And only a little blood
   wept
   on the ground.

Truth

He left, infallible, the door itself
                    was bruised as he
                    hit the mark.
We two sat awhile
                    the figures in the documents
                    staring at us like
                    green huge-headed beetles
                    out of the crevices of evening.
The books stretched
                    their spines,
the balance weighed just for the fun of it
                    and the glass beads in the necklace
                    of the god of sleep whispered together
                    in the scales.

'Have you ever been right?' one of us asked.
'I haven't.'

Then we counted on.
It was late
And outside the smokey town, frosty and purple, climbed to
    the stars.

PART TWO

Love

Two thousand cigarettes.
A hundred miles
from wall to wall.
An eternity and a half of vigils
blanker than snow.

Tons of words
old as the tracks
of a platypus in the sand.

A hundred books we didn't write.
A hundred pyramids we didn't build.

Sweepings.
Dust.

Bitter
as the beginning of the world.

Believe me when I say
it was beautiful.

Ode to Joy

You only love
when you love in vain.

Try another radio probe
when ten have failed,
take two hundred rabbits
when a hundred have died:
only this is science.

You ask the secret.
It has just one name:
again.

In the end
a dog carries in his jaws
his image in the water,
people rivet the new moon,
I love you.

Like caryatids
our lifted arms
hold up time's granite load

and defeated
we shall always win.

Death in the Evening

High, high.

Her last words wandered across the ceiling
like clouds.
The sideboard wept.
The apron shivered
as if covering an abyss.

The end. The young ones had gone to bed.

But towards midnight
the dead woman got up,
put out the candles (a pity to waste them),
quickly mended the last stocking,
found her fifty nickels
in the cinnamon tin
and put them on the table,
found the scissors fallen behind the cupboard,
found a glove
they had lost a year ago,
tried all the door knobs,
tightened the tap,
finished her coffee,
and fell back again.

In the morning they took her away.
She was cremated.
The ashes were coarse
as coal.

Five Minutes After the Air Raid

In Pilsen,
Twenty-six Station Road,
she climbed to the Third Floor
up stairs which were all that was left
of the whole house,
she opened her door
full on to the sky,
stood gaping over the edge.

For this was the place
the world ended.

Then
she locked up carefully
lest someone steal
Sirius
or Aldebaran
from her kitchen,
went back downstairs
and settled herself
to wait
for the house to rise again
and for her husband to rise from the ashes
and for her children's hands and feet to be stuck
    back in place.

In the morning they found her
still as stone,
sparrows pecking her hands.

Harbour

But the sea was measured
and chained to the earth.
And the earth was measured
and chained to the sea.

They launched
cranes, lean angels,
they calculated
the wail of widowed sirens,
they foresaw
the nervous unrest of buoys,
they drafted
the labyrinth of routes around the world.

They constructed
the Minotaurs of ships.

They discovered five continents.

The earth was measured
and chained to the sea.
And the sea was measured
and chained to the earth.

All that is left
is a small house above the canal.
A man who spoke softly,
a woman with tears in her eyes.
All that is left is the evening lamp,
the continent of the table,
the tablecloth, a sea-gull that does not fly away.

All that is left
is a cup of tea,
the deepest ocean in the world.

The Forest

Among the primary rocks
where the bird spirits
crack the granite seeds
and the tree statues
with their black arms
threaten the clouds,

suddenly
there comes a rumble,
as if history
were being uprooted,

the grass bristles,
boulders tremble,
the earth's surface cracks

and there grows

a mushroom,

immense as life itself,
filled with billions of cells
immense as life itself,
eternal,
watery,

appearing in this world for the first

and last time.

Waiting

The one who waits is always the mother,
all her fingers jammed
  in the automatic doors of the world,
all her thoughts like
  egg-laden moths pinned out alive,
and in her bag the mirror shows
  time long gone by when
  glad cries lingered in the apple trees,
and at home the spool and the thread are whispering together:
  What will become of us?

The one who waits is always the mother,
and a thousand things whose fate is
  ineluctable fall.

The one who waits is always the mother,
  smaller and smaller,
  fading and fading
  second by second,
until in the end
  no one sees her.

Fairy Tale

He built himself a house,
        his foundations,
        his stones,
        his walls,
        his roof overhead,
        his chimney and smoke,
        his view from the window.

He made himself a garden,
        his fence,
        his thyme,
        his earthworm,
        his evening dew.

He cut out his bit of sky above.

And he wrapped the garden in the sky
and the house in the garden
and packed the lot in a handkerchief

and went off
lone as an arctic fox
through the cold
unending
rain
into the world.

Water Sprite

You just have to
 start blowing bubbles underwater from the crack of dawn,
 stir up ripples all the morning,
 at noontime run the water off your coat-tails on the
  strips between the fields,
 all afternoon tread the mud in wavy ridges,
 at dusk start croaking at the moon, –

No one has the time today
just to sit and do a little haunting.

Lovers in August

Your hand travelled
   the Aztec trail
   down my breast.
The sun popped out like the egg
   of a platypus
and aspens pattered
   their leafy Ur-language.
All this has happened before.

The jellied landscape
   was furrowed with happiness.
You worshipped me
   like the goddess of warm rain.

But in each corner of our eyes
   stood one of Maxwell's demons
loosening the molecules
   of rise and fall
back and forth.

And in and out, round and about,
   in and out,
through the cracked lens of the eye
   unendingly,
   surface behind glass
   entropy mounted
   in the random and senseless universe.

All this has happened before.
All this will happen again.

Night at the Observatory

It was thawing.
As if the Avars
were attacking underground.

They stood leaning in the shadows,
his finger discovered
an inch
of unknown gentle country
beneath her left shoulder,

Atlantis, he said,
Atlantis.

Above the fields the wires hissed like iguanas.
A car's horn faded on the air
like a voice from Greek tragedy.
Behind the walls the guard paced back and forth.
Hares were sniffing the distant town.
Wood rotted in the ground.
The Avars were winning.
Trees cracked at the joints.
The wind came and veered off.
They kissed.

From somewhere a rock was falling
its second thousand years.
And the stars were taking in
signals on a frequency of ten megacycles,
beamed to a civilization
which had died
just before the dawn
of eternity.

Advent

Ice-floes lie along the river
like disused
wrappings
of life.

The church on the common is falling apart,
the vestry is leaking,
the altar candles are snuffling.

The Lord Himself has got the shivers.

He creeps
into the hen-house across the way
and sits nodding on the roost.

He lays no eggs,
nor does he crow.

Ice-floes lie along the river
like disused
wrappings
of life.

Night in the Streets

They are singing
at the bird-fancier's.
The houses are growing.

A few bricks
are coming away from the cathedral.
Here and there
a feather
or a cat
or dog
falls from the sky.

They are singing
at the bird-fancier's.

The houses are growing.
In their walls runs
the white blood of the just.
On the breath of millions
the moon rises,
the immense heart
rolls night towards day.

It's enough that we are alive.
Are breathing.

Responsible
even for the rotation of the earth.

Fog

The last road has fallen.
From every corner of the breathing fields
the triumphant sea draws nearer
and rocks in its waves
the voices of goldfinches
and the voices of the town.

We are a long way
from space and time,
we come upon the bobbing silhouettes
of stray dinosaurs
and the rayed shadows of Martians
who cannot see for fear.

You have something more to say, but
I do not understand you:
between us stretches
the enormous body of reality
and from its severed head
bubble the clots
of white blood.

The Rain at Night

With mouse-like teeth
the rain gnaws at stone.
The trees parade through the town
like prophets.

Perhaps it's the sobbing
of the monstrous angels of darkness,
perhaps the suppressed laughter
of the flowers out there in the garden,
trying to cure consumption
by rustling.

Perhaps the purring
of the holy drought
under any kind of cover.

An unspeakable time,
when the voice of loudspeakers cracks
and poems
are made not of words
but of drops.

The Wind in Winter

For too long have we stretched the bowstring of air.

All night we heard the menacing
grumble of engines,
we brought in the wind.

Then it happened. The heap toppled
and layer after layer
pack after pack
the snow dogs tumble,
their howls flogging the fields,

the wind returns, the rubber wind
brings back
the night and darkness
the sky and memory.

Thus we are alone, stripped of the landscape,
the last remnant of air in our lungs
and an evil laugh on our lips.

Such an evil laugh.

The Cat

Outside it was night
like a book without letters.
And the eternal dark
dripped to the stars through the sieve of the city.

I said to her
do not go
you'll only be trapped
and bewitched
and will suffer in vain.

I said to her
do not go
why want
nothing?

But a window was opened
and she went,

a black cat into the black night,
she dissolved,
a black cat in the black night,
she just dissolved

and no one ever saw her again.
Not even she herself.

But you can hear her
sometimes,
when it's quiet
and there's a northerly wind
and you listen intently
to your own self.

A Boy's Head

In it there is a space-ship
and a project
for doing away with piano lessons.

And there is
Noah's ark,
which shall be first.

And there is
an entirely new bird,
an entirely new hare,
an entirely new bumble-bee.

There is a river
that flows upwards.

There is a multiplication table.

There is anti-matter.

And it just cannot be trimmed.

I believe
that only what cannot be trimmed
is a head.

There is much promise
in the circumstance
that so many people have heads.

On the Building Site of a Hostel

Among pools of earth,
in a chain reaction of bricks,
between the decaying milk-teeth of concrete blocks

has just been hatched
a grey, two-phase
coffin.

(Wipe your feet)

Enter
a dignified museum
of the gall stones
of emptiness.

(Quiet please)

Fingers of piping explore the hollows
and the Monday morning howl
is everywhere.

(No spitting)

Above the bunk
a single bulb rages
suspended
from a concrete sky.

And on a nail
driven into flesh
shipwrecked socks and brassières
are drying.

(No sliding in the corridors)

We met
staring girls' eyes,
wandering like bugs over the plaster
and we asked,
what is love
and
shall we soon be young?

Prince Hamlet's Milk Tooth

His tooth fell out milky as
    a dandelion
and everything began to fall,
    as if a rosary had broken,
    as if the string of time had snapped,
and it was downhill going all the way;
round the corner the hearse-driver's coming from his dinner
blind horse in the lead, he jolts along.
Hamlet, we're on our way.

No time now except quickly
    learn to add and multiply,
    learn to cheat and whisper answers,
    to smoke and make love,
    lay in stocks of permanganate
    and naphthalene,
there won't be any more.
And we're on our way, Hamlet.

At dusk you hear the drunken revels of the Danes
    and the trampling of the pollinated flowers,
at dawn the typewriters tap out
    piles of loyalty checks
    with skeleton fingers,
at noon the paper tigers roar
    and commissions are counting up races,
    what will be left for seed
    when it falls.
Hamlet, we're on our way.

But we'll put a bird on our heads
    instead of a soldier's cap, won't we?
We shall walk through the park

and in the shadow of a red rock
('come in under the shadow of this red rock')
    we shall learn
    to think it over
    just in a small way,
    the way the moss grows,
    the way the wash-tubs soak up water,
or we'll take a walk
    five minutes beyond the town,
    growing smaller and smaller,
    a pace-maker on our hearts
    set to an easy rhythm
so we can eat our cake and have it too,
we'll take the oath a little
    and lie a little,
    just from want of not lying,
we heroic lads, salt of the earth,
with our muddled hopes
that one fine day
    we'll damn well prove our salt,
Hamlet.

And keep that tooth of yours.
There won't be any more.

How to Paint a Perfect Christmas

Above, you paint the sky
delicate as maidenhair.
Below, pour a little darkness
heated to room temperature
or slightly more.

With a cat's claw in the dark
scratch out a little tree,
the finest tree in the world,
finer than any forester
could ever imagine.

And the tree itself
will light up
and the whole picture purr
with green joy,
with purple hope.

Right. But now you must
put under the tree
the
real big thing,
the thing you most want in the world;
the thing pop-singers
call happiness.

It's easy enough for a cat,
a cat will put a mouse there,
Colonel Blimp will line up
the largest jet-propelled halberd
which shoots and bangs and salutes,
a sparrow will gather
a few stalks for its nest,

mister junior clerk will submit
a stuffed file tied with red tape,
a butterfly will put there
a new rubber peacock's eye,
but what will *you* put there?

You think and think
till the day grows grey,
till the river almost runs out,
till even the bulbs begin to yawn,
you think

and finally

there in the darkness you blot out
a hazy white spot,
a bit like a florin,
a bit like a ship,
a bit like the Moon,
a bit like the beautiful face
of someone (who?) else,

a hazy white spot,
perhaps more like emptiness,
like the negation of something,
like non-pain,
like non-fear,
like non-worry,

a hazy white spot,
and you go to bed
and say to yourself,
yes, now I know how to do it,
yes, now I know,

yes,
next time
I shall paint
the most perfect Christmas
that ever was.

The Door

Go and open the door.
  Maybe outside there's
  a tree, or a wood,
  a garden,
  or a magic city.

Go and open the door.
  Maybe a dog's rummaging.
  Maybe you'll see a face,
or an eye,
or the picture
            of a picture.

Go and open the door.
  If there's a fog
  it will clear.

Go and open the door.
  Even if there's only
  the darkness ticking,
  even if there's only
  the hollow wind,
  even if
            nothing
                  is there,
go and open the door.

At least
there'll be
a draught.

Riders

Over the kind earth twisted like Christmas-bread
over the white earth inscribed grammatically

in nonpareil, brevier, pica,
over the wise earth resounding
like the skull of St Augustine,
over the earth smooth as satin
shrouding the bosom of mystery,

four riders are galloping
on plump white horses,
four rosy-cheeked riders with forget-me-not eyes,
with velvet hands,
with lyres, sugar-basins,
and classics,

one of them lectures,
another one makes love,
the third sings praises,
the fourth gazes into the distance.

The earth undulates slightly behind them,
like the skin of a water snake,
and in the marks of their hooves
grey smallpox erupts.

These will be
the four riders
of the Apocalypse.

And What's New?

And what's new in the snow?
The tracks run apart.
Golden stains, purple stains,
like the fleece of a slaughtered lamb.

And what's new in the sand?
Cities in the distance,
a statue sticks out of each.
Some Lot's wife
looking back
slowly turns to stone.

And what's new in the mirror?
Breasts like young calves,
roes that are twins.
And Solomon the king
who is lying.

And what's new within?
Like the needle of a galvanometer,
like the source of a river
someone laughs airily.
And therefore is.

PART THREE

Textbook of a Dead Language

This is a boy.
This is a girl.

The boy has a dog.
The girl has a cat.

What colour is the dog?
What colour is the cat?

The boy and the girl
are playing with a ball.

Where is the ball rolling?

Where is the boy buried?
Where is the girl buried?

Read
and translate
into every silence and every language!

Write
where you yourselves
are buried!

The Village Green

The memorial of our heroes
has crumbled into stone:
the last casualty of the last war.

The sky over that spot
is healing the scar,
the goose fanfare
calls the wounded sward back to life.

But under the ground a mouse
says to another,
about to give birth:
Not here, come a bit farther!

The Lesson

A tree enters and says with a bow:
  I am a tree.
A black tear falls from the sky and says:
  I am a bird.

Down a spider's web
  something like love
    comes near
      and says:
  I am silence.

But by the blackboard sprawls
  a national democratic
  horse in his waistcoat
  and repeats,
  pricking his ears on every side,
  repeats and repeats
    I am the engine of history
    and
    we all
    love
    progress
    and
    courage
    and
    the fighters' wrath.

Under the classroom door
trickles
a thin stream of blood.

For here begins
the massacre
of the innocents.

Žito the Magician

To amuse His Royal Majesty he will change water into wine.
Frogs into footmen. Beetles into bailiffs. And make a Minister
out of a rat. He bows, and daisies grow from his finger-tips.
And a talking bird sits on his shoulder.

There.

Think up something else, demands His Royal Majesty.
Think up a black star. So he thinks up a black star.
Think up dry water. So he thinks up dry water.
Think up a river bound with straw-bands. So he does.

There.

Then along comes a student and asks: Think up sine alpha
greater than one.

And Žito grows pale and sad: Terribly sorry. Sine is
between plus one and minus one. Nothing you can do about
   that.
And he leaves the great royal empire, quietly weaves his way
through the throng of courtiers, to his home
                                        in a nutshell.

Inventions

Wise men in long white togas come forward during the
festivities, rendering account of their labours,
and King Belos listens.

O, mighty King, says the first, I've made a pair of wings
for your throne. You shall rule from the air. –
Then applause and cheering follow, the man is
richly rewarded.

O, mighty King, says the second, I've made a self-acting
dragon which will automatically defeat your foes. –
Then applause and cheering follow, the man is
richly rewarded.

O, mighty King, says the third, I've made a destroyer
of bad dreams. Now nothing shall disturb your royal sleep. –
Then applause and cheering follow, the man is
richly rewarded.

But the fourth man only says: Constant failure has dogged
my steps this year. Nothing went right. I bungled everything
I touched. – Horrified silence follows and
the wise King Belos is silent too.

It was ascertained later that the fourth man was
Archimedes.

A History Lesson

Kings
like golden gleams
made with a mirror on the wall.

A non-alcoholic pope,
knights without arms,
arms without knights.

The dead like so many strained noodles,
a pound of those fallen in battle,
two ounces of those who were executed,

several heads
like so many potatoes
shaken into a cap –

Geniuses conceived
by the mating of dates
are soaked up by the ceiling into infinity

to the sound of tinny thunder,
the rumble of bellies,
shouts of hurrah,

empires rise and fall
at a wave of the pointer,
the blood is blotted out –

And only one small boy,
who was not paying the least attention,
will ask
between two victorious wars:

And did it hurt in those days too?

Polonius

Behind every arras
he does his duty
unswervingly.
Walls are his ears,
keyholes his eyes.

He slinks up the stairs,
oozes from the ceiling,
floats through the door
ready to give evidence,
prove what is proven,
stab with a needle
or pin on an order.

His poems always rhyme,
his brush is dipped in honey,
his music flutes
from marzipan and cane.

You buy him
by weight, boneless,
a pound of wax flesh,
a pound of mousy philosophy,
a pound of jellied
flunkey.

And when he's sold out
and the left-overs wrapped
in a tasselled obituary,
a paranoid funeral notice,

and when the spore-creating mould
of memory

covers him over,
when he falls
arse-first to the stars,

the whole continent will be lighter,
earth's axis straighten up
and in night's thunderous arena
a bird will chirp in gratitude.

The Fly

She sat on a willow-trunk
watching
part of the battle of Crécy,
the shouts,
the gasps,
the groans,
the tramping and the tumbling.

During the fourteenth charge
of the French cavalry
she mated
with a brown-eyed male fly
from Vadincourt.

She rubbed her legs together
as she sat on a disembowelled horse
meditating
on the immortality of flies.

With relief she alighted
on the blue tongue
of the Duke of Clervaux.

When silence settled
and only the whisper of decay
softly circled the bodies

and only
a few arms and legs
still twitched jerkily under the trees,

she began to lay her eggs
on the single eye

of Johann Uhr,
the Royal Armourer.

And thus it was
that she was eaten by a swift
fleeing
from the fires of Estrées.

Fall of Troy

From burning Troy we took away
these rags of ours,
teeth in a glass
and a tattooed grandpa.

A bit further on the ancient quail
were nesting again
and silver pike were milting
in the quiet sky.

Nailed to the ground by a lance
a soldier
flapped a hand at us.
The wormwood spoke no word
nor did the gentian.

Just like home, said grandpa.

The bleating of lambs
arched a roof
over our heads.
The land flowed with manna.
From the time of the primary rocks
nothing had happened in fact.

And like a fingernail
grown into the flesh
our truth
was always with us.

We slept embraced,
rags wrapped about us,
teeth in a glass.
Just like home, said grandpa.

Nothing had happened in fact.
Only we understood
that Troy
      perhaps
            had really
fallen.

Discobolus

But
before his final throw
someone whispered to him
from behind
   – Just a moment,
   we still have to discuss this
   purely as a matter of form,
   – You don't know the situation,
   comrade,

   In principle we welcome
   your initiative,
   but you must understand

   – We have to insist on
   fundamental
   agreement
   for every throw,

he felt
the soft Sudanese reed
wind round his wrist,
he wanted to cry out
but
his mouth
was suddenly filled
with the candy-floss of the evening sky,
his muscles swelled
like Thessalian granite,
yet
there was really no point in it,
   – Forward there,
   someone said,
   make way, please,

Demosthenes
will throw now,
and Demosthenes
took a grain of sand from under his tongue
and neatly
flicked it in the other's eye,

– Hurrah, one more
world record,
they shouted,

desperate maddened nameless
Discobolus
again swung down
low from the knees,
but he was
already stone
and saw
only a single
huge grain of sand
from horizon to horizon.

So he stood there.

And round the corner
came
the first school excursions
led
by the finest pedagogues,
who referred especially
to the play of the shoulders,
the courageous human heart
and the proud pace forward
on the way
to eternity.

PART FOUR

A Dog in the Quarry

The day was so bright
  that even birdcages flew open.
The breasts of lawns
  heaved with joy
and the cars on the highway
  sang the great song of asphalt.
At Lobzy a dog fell in the quarry
  and howled.
Mothers pushed their prams out of the park opposite
because babies cannot sleep
  when a dog howls,
and a fat old pensioner was cursing the Municipality:
they let the dog fall in the quarry and then leave him there,
and this, if you please, has been going on since morning.

Towards evening even the trees
  stopped blossoming
and the water at the bottom of the quarry
  grew green with death.
But still the dog howled.

Then along came some boys
and made a raft out of two logs
and two planks.
And a man left on the bank
  a briefcase, in which bread is planted
  in the morning
so that by noon
  crumbs may sprout in it
(the kind of briefcase in which documents
  and deeds
  would die of cramp),
he laid aside his briefcase
and sailed with them.

Their way led across a green puddle
to the island where the dog waited.
It was a voyage like
   the discovery of America,
a voyage like
   the quest of Theseus.
The dog fell silent,
   the boys stood like statues
and one of them punted with a stick,
the waves shimmered nervously,
tadpoles swiftly
   flickered out of the wake,
the heavens
   stood still,
and the man stretched out his hand.

It was a hand
   reaching out across the ages,
it was a hand
   linking
   one world with another,
   life with death,
it was a hand
   joining everything together,
it caught the dog by the scruff of its neck

and then they sailed back
to the music of
an immense fanfare
of the dog's yapping.

It was not a question of that one dog.

It was not a question of that park.

Somehow it was a question
of our whole childhood,
   all of whose mischiefs
   will eventually out,
of all our loves,
of all the places we loved in
   and parted never to meet again,
of every prospect
   happy as grass,
unhappy as bone,
of every path up or down,
of every raft and all the other machines
we search for at our lathes
   and drawing-boards,
of everything we are reaching out for
round the corner of the landscape.

It was not an answer.

There are days when no answer is needed.

Planning

Around the table,
from hand to hand,
from file to file,
from column to column,
march

the refrigerators that are and
the refrigerators that will be,
white and gleaming
like an antarctic flotilla,

the preserves that are and
the preserves that will be,
red and green,
splendid as the pages
of the king of the glass castle,

the excavators that are and
the excavators that will be,
black and heroic
as a storm in a teacup,

the new-born that are and
the new-born that will be,
with bulging eyes
and a temporary shortage
of dummies,

march
fluorescent lamps,
books of poetry,
telescopes,
overcoats,
moulds,

megawatts
          precise as a surgical needle,
megatons
          certain as next spring,
march
around the table
in the cold dry glow
of cigarettes,
and the gradual welding
of fantasy
          with the steel bars of numbers.

The future
          to three decimal points
          exactly.

But sometimes,
when all's finished and signed,
the excavators,
the new-born,
the apples,
the books,
the refrigerators
pipe up
just for the heck of it,
without a reference number,
in quiet urgent voices –

and what about yourselves, friends,
what about yourselves,
to how many decimal points exactly,

your goodselves today,
your goodselves tomorrow,
to how many points exactly

at home
and in the street,
and with your wife
and your friends,
and morning
and evening,
and on the way up
and on the way down,
to how many decimal points exactly
you yourselves, friends?

And we should have an answer to that
in this year's plan.

Man Cursing the Sea

Someone
just climbed to the top of the cliff
and started cursing the sea:

Stupid water, stupid pregnant water,
slimy copy of the sky,
hesitant hoverer between the sun and the moon,
pettifogging reckoner of shells,
fluid, loud-mouthed bull,
fertilizing the rocks with his blood,
suicidal sword
splintering itself on any promontory,
hydra, fragmenting the night,
breathing salty clouds of silence,
spreading jelly-like wings
in vain, in vain,
gorgon, devouring its own body,

water, you absurd flat skull of water –

Thus for a while he cursed the sea,
which licked his footprints in the sand
like a wounded dog.

And then he came down
and stroked
the small immense stormy mirror of the sea.

There you are, water, he said,
and went his way.

Secrecy

You think it's a street,
  but it's only an arm-less sleeve.
You think it's joy,
  but it's only the clamour of the phone
  in an empty room.
You think it's sleep,
  but it's only the unending contortion
  of neurons in a brocade box.
You think it's a story,
  but it's only a summons.

And there, at the source of the rains, sits
  a chicken-headed judge,
In an arm-chair made of the tanned hide of philosophers,
  in a fly-blown aureole,
In music reduced to a mere wail,
  in light dimmed
  to electric shocks.

– All this for the purposes of secrecy –

At the source of the rains sits
  a chicken-headed judge
Holding
  the imperial globe of darkness,
Inside which there is
  a larger globe
Of half-shadow.

Model of Man

There is always somewhere some bundle
  giving off a little smoke, a little blood,
  a little wailing and a little singing,
  you can hear the trampling of feet, the
  flutter of flags,
  a button rolls away, or perhaps a head,
  or something,
  somebody laughs,
  somebody vomits,
  somebody says, oh, what's the use, let's go
    'n have a drink,
  somebody says, hurrah,
  somebody says, why, when I was young,
  somebody says, things were different . . . ,
  the bundle closes,
  and again there is a clatter, like when
  teeth are being knocked out or someone's
    knocking on wood,
  the clay twitches like a run-over dog –

And here someone's leaving,
Hit by lightning or by a pin,
Hit by an eight-pound stone,
Hit by a word,
Hit by a stick,
Hit by a neutron,
Hit by stupidity,
Hit by a poisoned arrow,
Hit by a dagger,
Hit by a kick in the pants,
Hit by a hundred times nothing.

He is a long time leaving, a night and a day,
  another two nights.

He dodges like a crazy raindrop,
Cowers like grass under a spray of water,

A Don Quixote grown wise,
A Roland grown quiet,
A general without badges of rank,
Limp and deflated like a statue of rags,
He seeks a hole, or a hospital or a museum,
But it's after six and everything's closed,
Windsor Castle
as well as the rat farm.

A knife at his back are
    his own eyes,
Like a heartbeat he keeps hearing
    his own voice –

What are they doing
Without me?

And so after those two nights
    and a day and a night

He turns
And goes there again.

Just for a while, he says.

But it's for a lifetime.

We don't know who he is.
Let's just call him
A man.

The Root of the Matter

Faust
or anyone
clumsy enough to be
    wise,
anyone who bends the nail
    at the first stroke,
anyone who forgets to buy
    his ticket or
    show his pass
  right at the start of the journey,
anyone who can be done out of an ounce
    of his half-pound of butter,
in short Faust
takes a walk
    (before Easter)
beyond the town, stepping into puddles
    he would have rather
    avoided,
strolls against the stream of passers-by, tags on to
    a crowd which
    is cheering, more or less, because
the weather's either cloudy or set fair
    and after all
There is nothing to do
except cheer
    strolls and shares their mood,
      finally
Some mistakes are now mistakes
others are still virtues
    walks around like a grandfather clock
      out of its case and forgetting to chime,

Nothing has happened but we
always saw it coming
    walks around like a run-down battery
          on a movable pavement,
    listens to the voices from above,
Birds of prey do not sing
    listens to the voices from below,
Are you looking for the meaning of life?
And how are you off for garlic?
    he takes the grey road past the cement works,
    he takes the red road past the slaughter-house,
    he takes the blue road past the lake,
    he takes the banned road past the council offices,
    he takes the green road past the playground
          yelling mindless bodies rolling on the ground –
Youth is no argument.
Age even less
    walks and thinks but rather just
          walks
Thinking is natural
only when there is nothing else
to do

II

And at last
    (naturally)
he meets a black poodle
    running around in smaller and
    smaller circles
like an ominous spider
    spinning its vast web.

  – Look, now we shall see
the poodle's true kernel,

the root of the matter,
says Faust and hurries off
home.
And the poodle circles
like a carrier raven,
For keeping one's balance
wings are best
like a cat, like a mouse,
like a black-burning bush,
There is poetry in everything. That
is the biggest argument
against poetry
like the ardent hump of the horizon
The hump and other survivals
of the past
and at the same moment the kindly stoniness of the
milestone,

Infallibility and other maladies
of adolescence
like the Marathon runner
and yet like himself
(*But the root of the matter is not*
in the matter itself)
like the demon that denies,
The more negative the type
the more often it says yes
like a fallen angel,
Fall and you shall not
be shaken
like the forefinger of the nether darkness.
But the root of the matter is not
in the matter itself
Faust hurries home,
the circles are growing smaller like the noose
tightening round the neck of a mystery.

And when Faust sees his house before him
he gropes for his always missing
          bunch of keys,
ready to make the sign of the cross,
Is the cross more human
than a straight line?
or the sign of the straight line,
From criticism of the straight line we get
the dash
or the sign of the heart,
How many organs are called
heart?
the sign of the heart on the palm,
Heart, yes, but where do we have
the palm?
As he's entering his house
and the poodle's crossing the street eager
as a stone about to become
          a star,
suddenly
like a knife that falls
          half-blade into the ground
a bus slips through
and
the poodle's run over and dies.

Faust has the cold shivers,
pushed out of history
by a grain of sand,
by a hundredweight of stupidity.

III
The root of the matter is not
in the matter itself

Grandma used to say
a man who makes no mistakes makes nothing
but some sort of termite always
        lurks in the kneading-trough
        of every holy eve

Faust lifts the poodle up
and the blood, like a chasuble put on
        over the head,
runs down at his feet

Keys chanced upon he goes and
opens the house and corridor
and study and the evening
confronting the cosmos.

And he sets down the poodle on his opened book
and the letters drink up the blood with gullets unassuaged
        for centuries,
and the pages suck it in through the skin of their
                                        unconsciousness

and it is like
a clown's red cap
on the flat skull of literature,
like a set of illuminated
        initials
after the letter Z.
*Howl! You won't have any
trouble with your spelling*

IV
Faust, without making light, since pain
        itself gives out the reflected light
        of death,
stands there, nonplussed, and says:

Dog and nothing but a dog,
who might have been the allegory of creation
and are no more than the very meaning of death,
who might have been the annunciator
of another and are no more than
crunched bones,

dog and nothing but a dog, black, white or other,
empty-handed messenger, because there is no
mystery
except the thread which from our hands
leads round the far side of things, round the collar
of the landscape
and up the sleeve of a star.
The root of the matter is not
in the matter itself
dog and nothing but a dog,
with your eyes gazing into
the sweet shell of terror,
stay, you are so fair.
Verweile doch, du bist
so schön
And Faust feels he loves the dog with a love
whose essence is hopelessness just as
hopelessness has its essence in love,
knows what he should do but cannot,
not having a bandage
nor
a veterinary's licence
nor
the right to redress the acts of omnibuses
The root of the matter is not
in the matter itself and often
not
in our hands

Faust merely knows.
In the distance a siren wails
    and bells die on the air,
it is long after Easter,
Wagner comes in
    to ask after his health,
The good man will live
so that on Judgment Day
he can discourse on the virtues
of naphthalene
    the dog is stretched out and his pupils
        span the horizon
    and the pages of the book beneath him quiver
        like white whispering lips.

And Faust knows
that he will not speak of it,
and if so only by a comma,
only by a word in a big new book.
It is really something like
    a coat of grey fur over the soul,
    like the uniform the unknown soldier
    wears inside him.

And so he goes and starts a painting,
or a gay little song,
or a big new book.
Nothing has happened but we
always saw it coming
    All in all India ink
        is the blood's first sister
    and song is just as final
        as life and death
    and equally without allegory,
        without transcendence
        and without fuss.

List of Translators

Poems translated by *George Theiner*:
A Helping Hand
Bones
Wings
'Heat with a Little Human
    Warmth'
Suffering
Pathology
Truth
Death in the Evening
Five Minutes After the Air Raid
Harbour
The Forest
The Rain at Night
The Wind in Winter
The Cat
On the Building Site of a Hostel
Riders
Textbook of a Dead Language
The Village Green
Žito the Magician
Inventions
A History Lesson
The Fly
A Dog in the Quarry
Man Cursing the Sea
Secrecy
Model of Man

Poems translated by *Ian Milner*:
In the Microscope
Reality
Silence
The Harp
Great and Strong
Love
Ode to Joy
Waiting
Fairy Tale
Water Sprite
Lovers in August
Night at the Observatory
Advent
Night in the Streets
Fog
A Boy's Head
Prince Hamlet's Milk Tooth
The Door
And What's New?
The Lesson
Polonius
Fall of Troy
Discobolus
Planning
The Root of the Matter

Translated by *George Theiner and Ian Milner*:
How to Paint a Perfect Christmas

MORE ABOUT PENGUINS

RIMBAUD

Edited by Oliver Bernard

Arthur Rimbaud (1854–91) ceased to write poetry at the age of nineteen, after publishing *Les Illuminations* and *Une Saison en Enfer* in 1872–3. His fiercely active literary career was marked by his association with Verlaine, which ended in a shooting affray.

In complete revolt against society and the values of the world, Rimbaud, as it were, carried on the work of Baudelaire. Even more spiritually isolated than Baudelaire, he went still further in his attempt to exalt poetry into a kind of sorcery. 'Je dis qu'il faut être *voyant*' ('I say that it is necessary to be a seer'), he wrote. Thus at times there is an extraordinary power of incantation in his verse, as if he would summon up in words a world to replace the world he rejected.

He later became a trader in Africa and the East, and his whole life and the poignant and tormented nature of his writing provides a curious literary riddle.

In this selection the French text is accompanied by English prose translations.

THE PENGUIN BOOK OF RUSSIAN VERSE

Edited by Dimitri Obolensky

The belief, current in the West, that Russian poetry
has its beginnings in the early nineteenth century
is, though misguided, understandable. The unex-
ampled blossoming of this poetry between 1810 and
1830, in a newly developed language easily recog-
nizable as modern Russian and in a literary context
avowedly European, makes the age of Pushkin
seem like a sudden flowering in a wilderness.
Eighteenth-century Russian literature, without
which Pushkin himself cannot be properly understood, is in the West largely unknown or dismissed
as derivative and 'pseudo-classical'; while further
back, the Russian Middle Ages extend in an ill-
defined penumbra, out of which inexplicably
emerge a number of heroic poems transmitted by
word of mouth from generation to generation,
some of which have been translated into languages
of Western Europe.

This collection of Russian verse, which extends
from heroic poems of the twelfth century to the
work of poets still living, is accompanied by plain
prose translations and an excellent introduction.

THE PENGUIN BOOK OF GERMAN VERSE

Edited by Leonard Forster

The Penguin Book of German Verse is the first attempt for many years to provide an anthology of German lyric poetry for the English public at large. Professor Forster's presentation is fresh and contemporary, and his range of selections extends from the Minnesingers – the German equivalent of the Troubadours – to established writers alive today. The prose translation at the foot of each page – a feature of Penguin anthologies – has encouraged him to include not only medieval poets, who would otherwise be difficult for readers equipped only with modern German to enjoy, but also some writers in dialect whose poems provide variety and exhibit a characteristic side of German literature.

Professor Forster has also given liberal space to the poets of the seventeenth century whose work has only comparatively recently come into favour in Germany itself and who correspond roughly to the English Metaphysical Poets, and he has supplemented his choice from that age with a handful of unforced folk-songs. For the later half of the book he has drawn freely on the acknowledged great: Goethe, Schiller, Hölderlin, Heine, Mörike, George, Rilke, Hofmannsthal, Trakl, Benn, and Brecht.

Penguin Modern European Poets

APOLLINAIRE SELECTED POEMS

Guillaume Apollinaire was a friend and supporter of the Cubists. His own experimental poetic forms employ rhythms which dispense with punctuation and a style of typography derived from exercises on postcards sent from the front in the First World War. Yet he is also in France the last of the poets whose lines young people know by heart.

YEVTUSHENKO: SELECTED POEMS

Yevgeny Yevtushenko is the fearless spokesman of his generation in Russia. In verse that is young, fresh, and outspoken he frets at restraint and injustice, as in his now famous protest over the Jewish pogrom at Kiev.

But he can write lyrically, too, of the simple things of humanity – love, a birthday, a holiday in Georgia. And in 'Zima Junction' he brilliantly records his impressions on a visit to his home in Siberia.